CONTENTS

NAME _____**AGE**_____

CONTACT NO_____

ADDRESS_____

_____

ALLERGIES_____

_____

PHYSICIAN_____

CONTACT NUMBER_____

ADDRESS_____

_____

EMERGENCY CONTACTS

CONTACT NUMBER_____

EMERGENCY CONTACT NAME_____

EMERGENCY CONTACT NUMBER_____

REGULAR MEDICATION

Year:	Month:		Week Commencing:						
Medication	Dose	**Mon**	**Tue**	**Wed**	**Thur**	**Fri**	**Sat**	**Sun**
	Frequency	Date ___	Date ___	Date ___	Date ___	Date ___	Date ___	Date ___
	Dose:	☐☐☐☐	☐☐☐☐	☐☐☐☐	☐☐☐☐	☐☐☐☐	☐☐☐☐	☐☐☐☐
	Frequency							
	Dose:	☐☐☐☐	☐☐☐☐	☐☐☐☐	☐☐☐☐	☐☐☐☐	☐☐☐☐	☐☐☐☐
	Frequency							

COMMENTS_____

_____

_____

_____

INSURANCE DETAILS

COMPANY

POLICY START DATE_____POLICY END DATE_____

COVER DETAILS_____

ADDRESS_____

_____

CONTACT NO:_____

EMAIL:_____

WEBSITE:_____

COMPANY

POLICY START DATE_____POLICY END DATE_____

COVER DETAILS_____

ADDRESS_____

_____

CONTACT NO:_____

EMAIL:_____

WEBSITE:_____

COMPANY

POLICY START DATE_____POLICY END DATE_____

COVER DETAILS_____

ADDRESS_____

_____

CONTACT NO:_____

EMAIL:_____

WEBSITE:_____

COMPANY

POLICY START DATE_____POLICY END DATE_____

COVER DETAILS_____

ADDRESS_____

_____

CONTACT NO:_____

EMAIL:_____

WEBSITE:_____

INSURANCE DETAILS

COMPANY

POLICY START DATE_____POLICY END DATE_____

COVER DETAILS_____

ADDRESS_____

_____

CONTACT NO:_____

EMAIL:_____

WEBSITE:_____

COMPANY

POLICY START DATE_____POLICY END DATE_____

COVER DETAILS_____

ADDRESS_____

_____

CONTACT NO:_____

EMAIL:_____

WEBSITE:_____

COMPANY

POLICY START DATE_____POLICY END DATE_____

COVER DETAILS_____

ADDRESS_____

_____

CONTACT NO:_____

EMAIL:_____

WEBSITE:_____

COMPANY

POLICY START DATE_____POLICY END DATE_____

COVER DETAILS_____

ADDRESS_____

_____

CONTACT NO:_____

EMAIL:_____

WEBSITE:_____

HEALTH CARE DETAILS

PEDIATRICIAN DETAILS

NAME:_____

ADDRESS:_____

_____

PHONE NUMBER_____

DENTIST

NAME:_____

ADDRESS:_____

_____

PHONE NUMBER_____

SPECIALIST

NAME:_____

ADDRESS:_____

_____

PHONE NUMBER_____

SPECIALIST

NAME:_____

ADDRESS:_____

_____

PHONE NUMBER_____

SPECIALIST

NAME:_____

ADDRESS:_____

_____

PHONE NUMBER_____

SPECIALIST

NAME:_____

ADDRESS:_____

_____

PHONE NUMBER_____

SPECIALIST

NAME:_____

ADDRESS:_____

_____

PHONE NUMBER_____

MEDICAL HISTORY

	YES	NO	COMMENTS
High Blood Pressure			
Diabetes			
Glaucoma			
Epilepsy			
Asthma			
Allergies			
High Cholesterol			
Cancer (type)			
Obesity			
Hearing Loss			
Stroke			
Drug Misuse			
Alcohol Misuse			
Kidney Problems			
Incontinent			
Ambulant			

EXTENDED MEDICAL INFORMATION

CAREGIVER INFORMATION

NAME_____

ORGANISATION_____

RELATIONSHIP_____

CONTACT NO:_____

EMAIL:_____

ADDRESS:_____

_____

_____

FREQUENCY OF VISITS	**Daily**		**Weekly**		**Fortnightly**		**Monthly**	

TYPE OF ASSISTANCE	Personal Care ☐	Domestic ☐	Meal Prep. ☐
	Medication ☐	Shopping ☐	Transportation ☐
	Appointments ☐	Paying Bills ☐	Other ☐

COMMENTS_____

_____

_____

_____

_____

_____

NAME_____

ORGANISATION_____

RELATIONSHIP_____

CONTACT NO:_____

EMAIL:_____

ADDRESS:_____

_____

_____

FREQUENCY OF VISITS	**Daily**		**Weekly**		**Fortnightly**		**Monthly**	

TYPE OF ASSISTANCE	Personal Care ☐	Domestic ☐	Meal Prep. ☐
	Medication ☐	Shopping ☐	Transportation ☐
	Appointments ☐	Paying Bills ☐	Other ☐

COMMENTS_____

_____

_____

_____

_____

_____

CAREGIVER INFORMATION

NAME_____

ORGANISATION_____

RELATIONSHIP_____

CONTACT NO:_____

EMAIL:_____

ADDRESS:_____

_____

_____

FREQUENCY OF VISITS	**Daily**		**Weekly**		**Fortnightly**		**Monthly**	

TYPE OF ASSISTANCE	Personal Care ☐	Domestic ☐	Meal Prep. ☐
	Medication ☐	Shopping ☐	Transportation ☐
	Appointments ☐	Paying Bills ☐	Other ☐

COMMENTS_____

_____

_____

_____

_____

_____

NAME_____

ORGANISATION_____

RELATIONSHIP_____

CONTACT NO:_____

EMAIL:_____

ADDRESS:_____

_____

_____

FREQUENCY OF VISITS	**Daily**		**Weekly**		**Fortnightly**		**Monthly**	

TYPE OF ASSISTANCE	Personal Care ☐	Domestic ☐	Meal Prep. ☐
	Medication ☐	Shopping ☐	Transportation ☐
	Appointments ☐	Paying Bills ☐	Other ☐

COMMENTS_____

_____

_____

_____

_____

_____

CAREGIVER INFORMATION

NAME_____

ORGANISATION_____

RELATIONSHIP_____

CONTACT NO:_____

EMAIL:_____

ADDRESS:_____

_____

_____

FREQUENCY OF VISITS	**Daily**		**Weekly**		**Fortnightly**		**Monthly**	

TYPE OF ASSISTANCE

Personal Care ☐		Domestic ☐		Meal Prep. ☐	
Medication ☐		Shopping ☐		Transportation ☐	
Appointments ☐		Paying Bills ☐		Other ☐	

COMMENTS_____

_____

_____

_____

_____

_____

NAME_____

ORGANISATION_____

RELATIONSHIP_____

CONTACT NO:_____

EMAIL:_____

ADDRESS:_____

_____

_____

FREQUENCY OF VISITS	**Daily**		**Weekly**		**Fortnightly**		**Monthly**	

TYPE OF ASSISTANCE

Personal Care ☐		Domestic ☐		Meal Prep. ☐	
Medication ☐		Shopping ☐		Transportation ☐	
Appointments ☐		Paying Bills ☐		Other ☐	

COMMENTS_____

_____

_____

_____

_____

_____

CAREGIVER INFORMATION

NAME_____

ORGANISATION_____

RELATIONSHIP_____

CONTACT NO:_____

EMAIL:_____

ADDRESS:_____

_____

_____

FREQUENCY OF VISITS	**Daily**		**Weekly**		**Fortnightly**		**Monthly**	

TYPE OF ASSISTANCE	Personal Care ☐	Domestic ☐	Meal Prep. ☐
	Medication ☐	Shopping ☐	Transportation ☐
	Appointments ☐	Paying Bills ☐	Other ☐

COMMENTS_____

_____

_____

_____

_____

_____

NAME_____

ORGANISATION_____

RELATIONSHIP_____

CONTACT NO:_____

EMAIL:_____

ADDRESS:_____

_____

_____

FREQUENCY OF VISITS	**Daily**		**Weekly**		**Fortnightly**		**Monthly**	

TYPE OF ASSISTANCE	Personal Care ☐	Domestic ☐	Meal Prep. ☐
	Medication ☐	Shopping ☐	Transportation ☐
	Appointments ☐	Paying Bills ☐	Other ☐

COMMENTS_____

_____

_____

_____

_____

_____

CAREGIVER INFORMATION

NAME_____

ORGANISATION_____

RELATIONSHIP_____

CONTACT NO:_____

EMAIL:_____

ADDRESS:_____

_____

_____

FREQUENCY OF VISITS	Daily		Weekly		Fortnightly		Monthly	

TYPE OF ASSISTANCE

Personal Care ☐   Domestic ☐   Meal Prep. ☐
Medication ☐   Shopping ☐   Transportation ☐
Appointments ☐   Paying Bills ☐   Other ☐

COMMENTS_____

_____

_____

_____

_____

_____

NAME_____

ORGANISATION_____

RELATIONSHIP_____

CONTACT NO:_____

EMAIL:_____

ADDRESS:_____

_____

_____

FREQUENCY OF VISITS	Daily		Weekly		Fortnightly		Monthly	

TYPE OF ASSISTANCE

Personal Care ☐   Domestic ☐   Meal Prep. ☐
Medication ☐   Shopping ☐   Transportation ☐
Appointments ☐   Paying Bills ☐   Other ☐

COMMENTS_____

_____

_____

_____

_____

_____

CAREGIVER INFORMATION

NAME_____

ORGANISATION_____

RELATIONSHIP_____

CONTACT NO:_____

EMAIL:_____

ADDRESS:_____

_____

_____

FREQUENCY OF VISITS	Daily		Weekly		Fortnightly		Monthly	

TYPE OF ASSISTANCE	Personal Care ☐	Domestic ☐	Meal Prep. ☐
	Medication ☐	Shopping ☐	Transportation ☐
	Appointments ☐	Paying Bills ☐	Other ☐

COMMENTS_____

_____

_____

_____

_____

_____

NAME_____

ORGANISATION_____

RELATIONSHIP_____

CONTACT NO:_____

EMAIL:_____

ADDRESS:_____

_____

_____

FREQUENCY OF VISITS	Daily		Weekly		Fortnightly		Monthly	

TYPE OF ASSISTANCE	Personal Care ☐	Domestic ☐	Meal Prep. ☐
	Medication ☐	Shopping ☐	Transportation ☐
	Appointments ☐	Paying Bills ☐	Other ☐

COMMENTS_____

_____

_____

_____

_____

_____

CAREGIVER INFORMATION

NAME_____

ORGANISATION_____

RELATIONSHIP_____

CONTACT NO:_____

EMAIL:_____

ADDRESS:_____

_____

_____

FREQUENCY OF VISITS	Daily		Weekly		Fortnightly		Monthly	

TYPE OF ASSISTANCE

Personal Care ☐	Domestic ☐	Meal Prep. ☐
Medication ☐	Shopping ☐	Transportation ☐
Appointments ☐	Paying Bills ☐	Other ☐

COMMENTS_____

_____

_____

_____

_____

_____

NAME_____

ORGANISATION_____

RELATIONSHIP_____

CONTACT NO:_____

EMAIL:_____

ADDRESS:_____

_____

_____

FREQUENCY OF VISITS	Daily		Weekly		Fortnightly		Monthly	

TYPE OF ASSISTANCE

Personal Care ☐	Domestic ☐	Meal Prep. ☐
Medication ☐	Shopping ☐	Transportation ☐
Appointments ☐	Paying Bills ☐	Other ☐

COMMENTS_____

_____

_____

_____

_____

_____

CAREGIVER INFORMATION

NAME_____

ORGANISATION_____

RELATIONSHIP_____

CONTACT NO:_____

EMAIL:_____

ADDRESS:_____

_____

_____

FREQUENCY OF VISITS	**Daily**		**Weekly**		**Fortnightly**		**Monthly**	

TYPE OF ASSISTANCE	Personal Care ☐	Domestic ☐	Meal Prep. ☐
	Medication ☐	Shopping ☐	Transportation ☐
	Appointments ☐	Paying Bills ☐	Other ☐

COMMENTS_____

_____

_____

_____

_____

_____

NAME_____

ORGANISATION_____

RELATIONSHIP_____

CONTACT NO:_____

EMAIL:_____

ADDRESS:_____

_____

_____

FREQUENCY OF VISITS	**Daily**		**Weekly**		**Fortnightly**		**Monthly**	

TYPE OF ASSISTANCE	Personal Care ☐	Domestic ☐	Meal Prep. ☐
	Medication ☐	Shopping ☐	Transportation ☐
	Appointments ☐	Paying Bills ☐	Other ☐

COMMENTS_____

_____

_____

_____

_____

_____

CAREGIVER TIMETABLE

CARER'S NAME

DATE							
TIME	MON	TUES	WED	THRS	FRI	SAT	SUN
BEGIN							
END							
TOTAL Hrs							

DATE							
TIME	MON	TUES	WED	THRS	FRI	SAT	SUN
BEGIN							
END							
TOTAL Hrs							

DATE							
TIME	MON	TUES	WED	THRS	FRI	SAT	SUN
BEGIN							
END							
TOTAL Hrs							

DATE							
TIME	MON	TUES	WED	THRS	FRI	SAT	SUN
BEGIN							
END							
TOTAL Hrs							

COMMENTS_____

_____

_____

_____

_____

CAREGIVER TIMETABLE

DATE							
TIME	MON	TUES	WED	THRS	FRI	SAT	SUN
BEGIN							
END							
TOTAL Hrs							

DATE							
TIME	MON	TUES	WED	THRS	FRI	SAT	SUN
BEGIN							
END							
TOTAL Hrs							

DATE							
TIME	MON	TUES	WED	THRS	FRI	SAT	SUN
BEGIN							
END							
TOTAL Hrs							

DATE							
TIME	MON	TUES	WED	THRS	FRI	SAT	SUN
BEGIN							
END							
TOTAL Hrs							

COMMENTS_____

_____

_____

_____

_____

CAREGIVER TIMETABLE

CARER'S NAME

DATE							
TIME	MON	TUES	WED	THRS	FRI	SAT	SUN
BEGIN							
END							
TOTAL Hrs							

DATE							
TIME	MON	TUES	WED	THRS	FRI	SAT	SUN
BEGIN							
END							
TOTAL Hrs							

DATE							
TIME	MON	TUES	WED	THRS	FRI	SAT	SUN
BEGIN							
END							
TOTAL Hrs							

DATE							
TIME	MON	TUES	WED	THRS	FRI	SAT	SUN
BEGIN							
END							
TOTAL Hrs							

COMMENTS_____

_____

_____

_____

_____

CAREGIVER TIMETABLE

CARER'S NAME

DATE							
TIME	MON	TUES	WED	THRS	FRI	SAT	SUN
BEGIN							
END							
TOTAL Hrs							

DATE							
TIME	MON	TUES	WED	THRS	FRI	SAT	SUN
BEGIN							
END							
TOTAL Hrs							

DATE							
TIME	MON	TUES	WED	THRS	FRI	SAT	SUN
BEGIN							
END							
TOTAL Hrs							

DATE							
TIME	MON	TUES	WED	THRS	FRI	SAT	SUN
BEGIN							
END							
TOTAL Hrs							

COMMENTS _____

_____

_____

_____

_____

CAREGIVER TIMETABLE

DATE							
TIME	MON	TUES	WED	THRS	FRI	SAT	SUN
BEGIN							
END							
TOTAL Hrs							

DATE							
TIME	MON	TUES	WED	THRS	FRI	SAT	SUN
BEGIN							
END							
TOTAL Hrs							

DATE							
TIME	MON	TUES	WED	THRS	FRI	SAT	SUN
BEGIN							
END							
TOTAL Hrs							

DATE							
TIME	MON	TUES	WED	THRS	FRI	SAT	SUN
BEGIN							
END							
TOTAL Hrs							

COMMENTS_____

_____

_____

_____

_____

CAREGIVER TIMETABLE

CARER'S NAME

DATE							
TIME	MON	TUES	WED	THRS	FRI	SAT	SUN
BEGIN							
END							
TOTAL Hrs							

DATE							
TIME	MON	TUES	WED	THRS	FRI	SAT	SUN
BEGIN							
END							
TOTAL Hrs							

DATE							
TIME	MON	TUES	WED	THRS	FRI	SAT	SUN
BEGIN							
END							
TOTAL Hrs							

DATE							
TIME	MON	TUES	WED	THRS	FRI	SAT	SUN
BEGIN							
END							
TOTAL Hrs							

COMMENTS_____

_____

_____

_____

_____

CAREGIVER TIMETABLE

CARER'S NAME

DATE							
TIME	MON	TUES	WED	THRS	FRI	SAT	SUN
BEGIN							
END							
TOTAL Hrs							

DATE							
TIME	MON	TUES	WED	THRS	FRI	SAT	SUN
BEGIN							
END							
TOTAL Hrs							

DATE							
TIME	MON	TUES	WED	THRS	FRI	SAT	SUN
BEGIN							
END							
TOTAL Hrs							

DATE							
TIME	MON	TUES	WED	THRS	FRI	SAT	SUN
BEGIN							
END							
TOTAL Hrs							

COMMENTS_____

_____

_____

_____

_____

CAREGIVER TIMETABLE

CARER'S NAME	

DATE							
TIME	MON	TUES	WED	THRS	FRI	SAT	SUN
BEGIN							
END							
TOTAL Hrs							

DATE							
TIME	MON	TUES	WED	THRS	FRI	SAT	SUN
BEGIN							
END							
TOTAL Hrs							

DATE							
TIME	MON	TUES	WED	THRS	FRI	SAT	SUN
BEGIN							
END							
TOTAL Hrs							

DATE							
TIME	MON	TUES	WED	THRS	FRI	SAT	SUN
BEGIN							
END							
TOTAL Hrs							

COMMENTS_____

_____

_____

_____

_____

CAREGIVER TIMETABLE

DATE							
TIME	MON	TUES	WED	THRS	FRI	SAT	SUN
BEGIN							
END							
TOTAL Hrs							

DATE							
TIME	MON	TUES	WED	THRS	FRI	SAT	SUN
BEGIN							
END							
TOTAL Hrs							

DATE							
TIME	MON	TUES	WED	THRS	FRI	SAT	SUN
BEGIN							
END							
TOTAL Hrs							

DATE							
TIME	MON	TUES	WED	THRS	FRI	SAT	SUN
BEGIN							
END							
TOTAL Hrs							

COMMENTS_____

_____

_____

_____

_____

CAREGIVER TIMETABLE

DATE							
TIME	MON	TUES	WED	THRS	FRI	SAT	SUN
BEGIN							
END							
TOTAL Hrs							

DATE							
TIME	MON	TUES	WED	THRS	FRI	SAT	SUN
BEGIN							
END							
TOTAL Hrs							

DATE							
TIME	MON	TUES	WED	THRS	FRI	SAT	SUN
BEGIN							
END							
TOTAL Hrs							

DATE							
TIME	MON	TUES	WED	THRS	FRI	SAT	SUN
BEGIN							
END							
TOTAL Hrs							

COMMENTS_____

_____

_____

_____

_____

CAREGIVER TIMETABLE

CARER'S NAME

DATE							
TIME	MON	TUES	WED	THRS	FRI	SAT	SUN
BEGIN							
END							
TOTAL Hrs							

DATE							
TIME	MON	TUES	WED	THRS	FRI	SAT	SUN
BEGIN							
END							
TOTAL Hrs							

DATE							
TIME	MON	TUES	WED	THRS	FRI	SAT	SUN
BEGIN							
END							
TOTAL Hrs							

DATE							
TIME	MON	TUES	WED	THRS	FRI	SAT	SUN
BEGIN							
END							
TOTAL Hrs							

COMMENTS_____

_____

_____

_____

_____

CAREGIVER TIMETABLE

DATE							
TIME	MON	TUES	WED	THRS	FRI	SAT	SUN
BEGIN							
END							
TOTAL Hrs							

DATE							
TIME	MON	TUES	WED	THRS	FRI	SAT	SUN
BEGIN							
END							
TOTAL Hrs							

DATE							
TIME	MON	TUES	WED	THRS	FRI	SAT	SUN
BEGIN							
END							
TOTAL Hrs							

DATE							
TIME	MON	TUES	WED	THRS	FRI	SAT	SUN
BEGIN							
END							
TOTAL Hrs							

COMMENTS_____

_____

_____

_____

_____

CAREGIVER TIMETABLE

CARER'S NAME

DATE							
TIME	MON	TUES	WED	THRS	FRI	SAT	SUN
BEGIN							
END							
TOTAL Hrs							

DATE							
TIME	MON	TUES	WED	THRS	FRI	SAT	SUN
BEGIN							
END							
TOTAL Hrs							

DATE							
TIME	MON	TUES	WED	THRS	FRI	SAT	SUN
BEGIN							
END							
TOTAL Hrs							

DATE							
TIME	MON	TUES	WED	THRS	FRI	SAT	SUN
BEGIN							
END							
TOTAL Hrs							

COMMENTS_____

_____

_____

_____

_____

CAREGIVER TIMETABLE

CARER'S NAME							

DATE							
TIME	**MON**	**TUES**	**WED**	**THRS**	**FRI**	**SAT**	**SUN**
BEGIN							
END							
TOTAL Hrs							

DATE							
TIME	**MON**	**TUES**	**WED**	**THRS**	**FRI**	**SAT**	**SUN**
BEGIN							
END							
TOTAL Hrs							

DATE							
TIME	**MON**	**TUES**	**WED**	**THRS**	**FRI**	**SAT**	**SUN**
BEGIN							
END							
TOTAL Hrs							

DATE							
TIME	**MON**	**TUES**	**WED**	**THRS**	**FRI**	**SAT**	**SUN**
BEGIN							
END							
TOTAL Hrs							

COMMENTS_____

_____

_____

_____

_____

SELF CARE ABILITIES

PERSONAL CARE	YES	NO	SUPPORT REQUIRED	COMMENTS
Brush Teeth				
Change Clothes				
Bathing				
Eating				
Grooming				
Shoes On/Off				
Mobility				
Toileting				

HOME CARE	YES	NO	SUPPORT REQUIRED	COMMENTS
Meal Prep				
Laundry				
Shopping				
Cleaning				
Transport				

SUPPORT REQUIRED

	YES	NO	SUPPORT REQUIRED	COMMENTS

	YES	NO	SUPPORT REQUIRED	COMMENTS

DAILY CARE LOG

NAME OF CARER_____DATE_____

TIME BEGIN_____TIME ENDED_____

SERVICE PROVIDED_____

MEDICATION	DOSE	TIME	COMMENTS

MEALS		TIME	QUANTITY
Breakfast			
Lunch			
Teatime			
Dinner			

TIME	ACTIVITIES

PERSONAL HYGIENE	TIME	COMMENTS

SUPPLIES NEEDED	PURCHASED	DETAILS

COMMENTS_____

_____

_____

DAILY CARE LOG

NAME OF CARER_____DATE_____
TIME BEGIN_____TIME ENDED_____
SERVICE PROVIDED_____

MEDICATION	DOSE	TIME	COMMENTS

MEALS		TIME	QUANTITY
Breakfast			
Lunch			
Teatime			
Dinner			

TIME	ACTIVITIES

PERSONAL HYGIENE	TIME	COMMENTS

SUPPLIES NEEDED	PURCHASED	DETAILS

COMMENTS_____
_____
_____

DAILY CARE LOG

NAME OF CARER_____DATE_____

TIME BEGIN_____TIME ENDED_____

SERVICE PROVIDED_____

MEDICATION	DOSE	TIME	COMMENTS

MEALS		TIME	QUANTITY
Breakfast			
Lunch			
Teatime			
Dinner			

TIME	ACTIVITIES

PERSONAL HYGIENE	TIME	COMMENTS

SUPPLIES NEEDED	PURCHASED	DETAILS

COMMENTS_____

_____

_____

DAILY CARE LOG

NAME OF CARER_____DATE_____
TIME BEGIN_____TIME ENDED_____
SERVICE PROVIDED_____
_____

MEDICATION	DOSE	TIME	COMMENTS

MEALS		TIME	QUANTITY
Breakfast			
Lunch			
Teatime			
Dinner			

TIME	ACTIVITIES

PERSONAL HYGIENE	TIME	COMMENTS

SUPPLIES NEEDED	PURCHASED	DETAILS

COMMENTS_____
_____
_____

DAILY CARE LOG

NAME OF CARER_____DATE_____

TIME BEGIN_____TIME ENDED_____

SERVICE PROVIDED_____

_____

MEDICATION	DOSE	TIME	COMMENTS

MEALS		TIME	QUANTITY
Breakfast			
Lunch			
Teatime			
Dinner			

TIME	ACTIVITIES

PERSONAL HYGIENE	TIME	COMMENTS

SUPPLIES NEEDED	PURCHASED	DETAILS

COMMENTS_____

_____

_____

DAILY CARE LOG

NAME OF CARER_____DATE_____
TIME BEGIN_____TIME ENDED_____
SERVICE PROVIDED_____
_____

MEDICATION	DOSE	TIME	COMMENTS

MEALS		TIME	QUANTITY
Breakfast			
Lunch			
Teatime			
Dinner			

TIME	ACTIVITIES

PERSONAL HYGIENE	TIME	COMMENTS

SUPPLIES NEEDED	PURCHASED	DETAILS

COMMENTS_____
_____
_____

DAILY CARE LOG

NAME OF CARER_____DATE_____
TIME BEGIN_____TIME ENDED_____
SERVICE PROVIDED_____
_____

MEDICATION	DOSE	TIME	COMMENTS

MEALS		TIME	QUANTITY
Breakfast			
Lunch			
Teatime			
Dinner			

TIME	ACTIVITIES

PERSONAL HYGIENE	TIME	COMMENTS

SUPPLIES NEEDED	PURCHASED	DETAILS

COMMENTS_____
_____
_____

DAILY CARE LOG

NAME OF CARER_____DATE_____
TIME BEGIN_____TIME ENDED_____
SERVICE PROVIDED_____

MEDICATION	DOSE	TIME	COMMENTS

MEALS		TIME	QUANTITY
Breakfast			
Lunch			
Teatime			
Dinner			

TIME	ACTIVITIES

PERSONAL HYGIENE	TIME	COMMENTS

SUPPLIES NEEDED	PURCHASED	DETAILS

COMMENTS_____
_____
_____

DAILY CARE LOG

NAME OF CARER_____DATE_____

TIME BEGIN_____TIME ENDED_____

SERVICE PROVIDED_____

MEDICATION	DOSE	TIME	COMMENTS

MEALS		TIME	QUANTITY
Breakfast			
Lunch			
Teatime			
Dinner			

TIME	ACTIVITIES

PERSONAL HYGIENE	TIME	COMMENTS

SUPPLIES NEEDED	PURCHASED	DETAILS

COMMENTS_____

_____

DAILY CARE LOG

NAME OF CARER_____DATE_____
TIME BEGIN_____TIME ENDED_____
SERVICE PROVIDED_____

MEDICATION	DOSE	TIME	COMMENTS

MEALS		TIME	QUANTITY
Breakfast			
Lunch			
Teatime			
Dinner			

TIME	ACTIVITIES

PERSONAL HYGIENE	TIME	COMMENTS

SUPPLIES NEEDED	PURCHASED	DETAILS

COMMENTS_____
_____
_____

DAILY CARE LOG

NAME OF CARER_____DATE_____

TIME BEGIN_____TIME ENDED_____

SERVICE PROVIDED_____

MEDICATION	DOSE	TIME	COMMENTS

MEALS		TIME	QUANTITY
Breakfast			
Lunch			
Teatime			
Dinner			

TIME	ACTIVITIES

PERSONAL HYGIENE	TIME	COMMENTS

SUPPLIES NEEDED	PURCHASED	DETAILS

COMMENTS_____

_____

_____

DAILY CARE LOG

NAME OF CARER_____DATE_____
TIME BEGIN_____TIME ENDED_____
SERVICE PROVIDED_____
_____

MEDICATION	DOSE	TIME	COMMENTS

MEALS		TIME	QUANTITY
Breakfast			
Lunch			
Teatime			
Dinner			

TIME	ACTIVITIES

PERSONAL HYGIENE	TIME	COMMENTS

SUPPLIES NEEDED	PURCHASED	DETAILS

COMMENTS_____
_____
_____

DAILY CARE LOG

NAME OF CARER_____DATE_____

TIME BEGIN_____TIME ENDED_____

SERVICE PROVIDED_____

MEDICATION	DOSE	TIME	COMMENTS

MEALS		TIME	QUANTITY
Breakfast			
Lunch			
Teatime			
Dinner			

TIME	ACTIVITIES

PERSONAL HYGIENE	TIME	COMMENTS

SUPPLIES NEEDED	PURCHASED	DETAILS

COMMENTS_____

_____

_____

DAILY CARE LOG

NAME OF CARER_____DATE_____

TIME BEGIN_____TIME ENDED_____

SERVICE PROVIDED_____

MEDICATION	DOSE	TIME	COMMENTS

MEALS		TIME	QUANTITY
Breakfast			
Lunch			
Teatime			
Dinner			

TIME	ACTIVITIES

PERSONAL HYGIENE	TIME	COMMENTS

SUPPLIES NEEDED	PURCHASED	DETAILS

COMMENTS_____

_____

_____

DAILY CARE LOG

NAME OF CARER_____DATE_____
TIME BEGIN_____TIME ENDED_____
SERVICE PROVIDED_____

MEDICATION	DOSE	TIME	COMMENTS

MEALS		TIME	QUANTITY
Breakfast			
Lunch			
Teatime			
Dinner			

TIME	ACTIVITIES

PERSONAL HYGIENE	TIME	COMMENTS

SUPPLIES NEEDED	PURCHASED	DETAILS

COMMENTS_____
_____
_____

DAILY CARE LOG

NAME OF CARER_____DATE_____
TIME BEGIN_____TIME ENDED_____
SERVICE PROVIDED_____

MEDICATION	DOSE	TIME	COMMENTS

MEALS		TIME	QUANTITY
Breakfast			
Lunch			
Teatime			
Dinner			

TIME	ACTIVITIES

PERSONAL HYGIENE	TIME	COMMENTS

SUPPLIES NEEDED	PURCHASED	DETAILS

COMMENTS_____
_____
_____

DAILY CARE LOG

NAME OF CARER_____DATE_____
TIME BEGIN_____TIME ENDED_____
SERVICE PROVIDED_____

MEDICATION	DOSE	TIME	COMMENTS

MEALS		TIME	QUANTITY
Breakfast			
Lunch			
Teatime			
Dinner			

TIME	ACTIVITIES

PERSONAL HYGIENE	TIME	COMMENTS

SUPPLIES NEEDED	PURCHASED	DETAILS

COMMENTS_____
_____
_____

DAILY CARE LOG

NAME OF CARER_____DATE_____
TIME BEGIN_____TIME ENDED_____
SERVICE PROVIDED_____

MEDICATION	DOSE	TIME	COMMENTS

MEALS		TIME	QUANTITY
Breakfast			
Lunch			
Teatime			
Dinner			

TIME	ACTIVITIES

PERSONAL HYGIENE	TIME	COMMENTS

SUPPLIES NEEDED	PURCHASED	DETAILS

COMMENTS_____
_____
_____

DAILY CARE LOG

NAME OF CARER_____DATE_____

TIME BEGIN_____TIME ENDED_____

SERVICE PROVIDED_____

MEDICATION	DOSE	TIME	COMMENTS

MEALS		TIME	QUANTITY
Breakfast			
Lunch			
Teatime			
Dinner			

TIME	ACTIVITIES

PERSONAL HYGIENE	TIME	COMMENTS

SUPPLIES NEEDED	PURCHASED	DETAILS

COMMENTS_____

_____

_____

DAILY CARE LOG

NAME OF CARER_____DATE_____
TIME BEGIN_____TIME ENDED_____
SERVICE PROVIDED_____

MEDICATION	DOSE	TIME	COMMENTS

MEALS		TIME	QUANTITY
Breakfast			
Lunch			
Teatime			
Dinner			

TIME	ACTIVITIES

PERSONAL HYGIENE	TIME	COMMENTS

SUPPLIES NEEDED	PURCHASED	DETAILS

COMMENTS_____
_____
_____

DAILY CARE LOG

NAME OF CARER_____DATE_____

TIME BEGIN_____TIME ENDED_____

SERVICE PROVIDED_____

_____

MEDICATION	DOSE	TIME	COMMENTS

MEALS		TIME	QUANTITY
Breakfast			
Lunch			
Teatime			
Dinner			

TIME	ACTIVITIES

PERSONAL HYGIENE	TIME	COMMENTS

SUPPLIES NEEDED	PURCHASED	DETAILS

COMMENTS_____

_____

_____

DAILY CARE LOG

NAME OF CARER_____DATE_____

TIME BEGIN_____TIME ENDED_____

SERVICE PROVIDED_____

MEDICATION	DOSE	TIME	COMMENTS

MEALS		TIME	QUANTITY
Breakfast			
Lunch			
Teatime			
Dinner			

TIME	ACTIVITIES

PERSONAL HYGIENE	TIME	COMMENTS

SUPPLIES NEEDED	PURCHASED	DETAILS

COMMENTS_____

_____

_____

DAILY CARE LOG

NAME OF CARER_____DATE_____

TIME BEGIN_____TIME ENDED_____

SERVICE PROVIDED_____

MEDICATION	DOSE	TIME	COMMENTS

MEALS		TIME	QUANTITY
Breakfast			
Lunch			
Teatime			
Dinner			

TIME	ACTIVITIES

PERSONAL HYGIENE	TIME	COMMENTS

SUPPLIES NEEDED	PURCHASED	DETAILS

COMMENTS_____

_____

_____

DAILY CARE LOG

NAME OF CARER_____DATE_____
TIME BEGIN_____TIME ENDED_____
SERVICE PROVIDED_____

MEDICATION	DOSE	TIME	COMMENTS

MEALS		TIME	QUANTITY
Breakfast			
Lunch			
Teatime			
Dinner			

TIME	ACTIVITIES

PERSONAL HYGIENE	TIME	COMMENTS

SUPPLIES NEEDED	PURCHASED	DETAILS

COMMENTS_____
_____
_____

DAILY CARE LOG

NAME OF CARER_____DATE_____

TIME BEGIN_____TIME ENDED_____

SERVICE PROVIDED_____

_____

MEDICATION	DOSE	TIME	COMMENTS

MEALS		TIME	QUANTITY
Breakfast			
Lunch			
Teatime			
Dinner			

TIME	ACTIVITIES

PERSONAL HYGIENE	TIME	COMMENTS

SUPPLIES NEEDED	PURCHASED	DETAILS

COMMENTS_____

_____

_____

DAILY CARE LOG

NAME OF CARER_____DATE_____

TIME BEGIN_____TIME ENDED_____

SERVICE PROVIDED_____

MEDICATION	DOSE	TIME	COMMENTS

MEALS		TIME	QUANTITY
Breakfast			
Lunch			
Teatime			
Dinner			

TIME	ACTIVITIES

PERSONAL HYGIENE	TIME	COMMENTS

SUPPLIES NEEDED	PURCHASED	DETAILS

COMMENTS_____

_____

DAILY CARE LOG

NAME OF CARER_____DATE_____
TIME BEGIN_____TIME ENDED_____
SERVICE PROVIDED_____
_____

MEDICATION	DOSE	TIME	COMMENTS

MEALS		TIME	QUANTITY
Breakfast			
Lunch			
Teatime			
Dinner			

TIME	ACTIVITIES

PERSONAL HYGIENE	TIME	COMMENTS

SUPPLIES NEEDED	PURCHASED	DETAILS

COMMENTS_____
_____
_____

DAILY CARE LOG

NAME OF CARER_____DATE_____
TIME BEGIN_____TIME ENDED_____
SERVICE PROVIDED_____
_____

MEDICATION	DOSE	TIME	COMMENTS

MEALS		TIME	QUANTITY
Breakfast			
Lunch			
Teatime			
Dinner			

TIME	ACTIVITIES

PERSONAL HYGIENE	TIME	COMMENTS

SUPPLIES NEEDED	PURCHASED	DETAILS

COMMENTS_____
_____
_____

DAILY CARE LOG

NAME OF CARER_____DATE_____
TIME BEGIN_____TIME ENDED_____
SERVICE PROVIDED_____

MEDICATION	DOSE	TIME	COMMENTS

MEALS		TIME	QUANTITY
Breakfast			
Lunch			
Teatime			
Dinner			

TIME	ACTIVITIES

PERSONAL HYGIENE	TIME	COMMENTS

SUPPLIES NEEDED	PURCHASED	DETAILS

COMMENTS_____
_____
_____

DAILY CARE LOG

NAME OF CARER_____DATE_____
TIME BEGIN_____TIME ENDED_____
SERVICE PROVIDED_____
_____

MEDICATION	DOSE	TIME	COMMENTS

MEALS		TIME	QUANTITY
Breakfast			
Lunch			
Teatime			
Dinner			

TIME	ACTIVITIES

PERSONAL HYGIENE	TIME	COMMENTS

SUPPLIES NEEDED	PURCHASED	DETAILS

COMMENTS_____
_____
_____

DAILY CARE LOG

NAME OF CARER_____DATE_____

TIME BEGIN_____TIME ENDED_____

SERVICE PROVIDED_____

MEDICATION	DOSE	TIME	COMMENTS

MEALS		TIME	QUANTITY
Breakfast			
Lunch			
Teatime			
Dinner			

TIME	ACTIVITIES

PERSONAL HYGIENE	TIME	COMMENTS

SUPPLIES NEEDED	PURCHASED	DETAILS

COMMENTS_____

_____

_____

DAILY CARE LOG

NAME OF CARER_____DATE_____

TIME BEGIN_____TIME ENDED_____

SERVICE PROVIDED_____
_____

MEDICATION	DOSE	TIME	COMMENTS

MEALS		TIME	QUANTITY
Breakfast			
Lunch			
Teatime			
Dinner			

TIME	ACTIVITIES

PERSONAL HYGIENE	TIME	COMMENTS

SUPPLIES NEEDED	PURCHASED	DETAILS

COMMENTS_____
_____
_____

DAILY CARE LOG

NAME OF CARER_____DATE_____
TIME BEGIN_____TIME ENDED_____
SERVICE PROVIDED_____

MEDICATION	DOSE	TIME	COMMENTS

MEALS		TIME	QUANTITY
Breakfast			
Lunch			
Teatime			
Dinner			

TIME	ACTIVITIES

PERSONAL HYGIENE	TIME	COMMENTS

SUPPLIES NEEDED	PURCHASED	DETAILS

COMMENTS_____
_____
_____

DAILY CARE LOG

NAME OF CARER_____DATE_____
TIME BEGIN_____TIME ENDED_____
SERVICE PROVIDED_____
_____

MEDICATION	DOSE	TIME	COMMENTS

MEALS		TIME	QUANTITY
Breakfast			
Lunch			
Teatime			
Dinner			

TIME	ACTIVITIES

PERSONAL HYGIENE	TIME	COMMENTS

SUPPLIES NEEDED	PURCHASED	DETAILS

COMMENTS_____
_____
_____

DAILY CARE LOG

NAME OF CARER_____DATE_____

TIME BEGIN_____TIME ENDED_____

SERVICE PROVIDED_____

MEDICATION	DOSE	TIME	COMMENTS

MEALS		TIME	QUANTITY
Breakfast			
Lunch			
Teatime			
Dinner			

TIME	ACTIVITIES

PERSONAL HYGIENE	TIME	COMMENTS

SUPPLIES NEEDED	PURCHASED	DETAILS

COMMENTS_____

_____

_____

DAILY CARE LOG

NAME OF CARER_____DATE_____
TIME BEGIN_____TIME ENDED_____
SERVICE PROVIDED_____
_____

MEDICATION	DOSE	TIME	COMMENTS

MEALS		TIME	QUANTITY
Breakfast			
Lunch			
Teatime			
Dinner			

TIME	ACTIVITIES

PERSONAL HYGIENE	TIME	COMMENTS

SUPPLIES NEEDED	PURCHASED	DETAILS

COMMENTS_____
_____
_____

DAILY CARE LOG

NAME OF CARER_____DATE_____
TIME BEGIN_____TIME ENDED_____
SERVICE PROVIDED_____

MEDICATION	DOSE	TIME	COMMENTS

MEALS		TIME	QUANTITY
Breakfast			
Lunch			
Teatime			
Dinner			

TIME	ACTIVITIES

PERSONAL HYGIENE	TIME	COMMENTS

SUPPLIES NEEDED	PURCHASED	DETAILS

COMMENTS_____
_____
_____

DAILY CARE LOG

NAME OF CARER_____DATE_____

TIME BEGIN_____TIME ENDED_____

SERVICE PROVIDED_____

MEDICATION	DOSE	TIME	COMMENTS

MEALS		TIME	QUANTITY
Breakfast			
Lunch			
Teatime			
Dinner			

TIME	ACTIVITIES

PERSONAL HYGIENE	TIME	COMMENTS

SUPPLIES NEEDED	PURCHASED	DETAILS

COMMENTS_____

_____

_____

DAILY CARE LOG

NAME OF CARER_____DATE_____

TIME BEGIN_____TIME ENDED_____

SERVICE PROVIDED_____

MEDICATION	DOSE	TIME	COMMENTS

MEALS		TIME	QUANTITY
Breakfast			
Lunch			
Teatime			
Dinner			

TIME	ACTIVITIES

PERSONAL HYGIENE	TIME	COMMENTS

SUPPLIES NEEDED	PURCHASED	DETAILS

COMMENTS_____

_____

_____

DAILY CARE LOG

NAME OF CARER_____DATE_____
TIME BEGIN_____TIME ENDED_____
SERVICE PROVIDED_____

MEDICATION	DOSE	TIME	COMMENTS

MEALS		TIME	QUANTITY
Breakfast			
Lunch			
Teatime			
Dinner			

TIME	ACTIVITIES

PERSONAL HYGIENE	TIME	COMMENTS

SUPPLIES NEEDED	PURCHASED	DETAILS

COMMENTS_____
_____
_____

DAILY CARE LOG

NAME OF CARER_____DATE_____

TIME BEGIN_____TIME ENDED_____

SERVICE PROVIDED_____

MEDICATION	DOSE	TIME	COMMENTS

MEALS		TIME	QUANTITY
Breakfast			
Lunch			
Teatime			
Dinner			

TIME	ACTIVITIES

PERSONAL HYGIENE	TIME	COMMENTS

SUPPLIES NEEDED	PURCHASED	DETAILS

COMMENTS_____

_____

_____

DAILY CARE LOG

NAME OF CARER_____DATE_____
TIME BEGIN_____TIME ENDED_____
SERVICE PROVIDED_____

MEDICATION	DOSE	TIME	COMMENTS

MEALS		TIME	QUANTITY
Breakfast			
Lunch			
Teatime			
Dinner			

TIME	ACTIVITIES

PERSONAL HYGIENE	TIME	COMMENTS

SUPPLIES NEEDED	PURCHASED	DETAILS

COMMENTS_____
_____
_____

DAILY CARE LOG

NAME OF CARER_____DATE_____
TIME BEGIN_____TIME ENDED_____
SERVICE PROVIDED_____
_____

MEDICATION	DOSE	TIME	COMMENTS

MEALS		TIME	QUANTITY
Breakfast			
Lunch			
Teatime			
Dinner			

TIME	ACTIVITIES

PERSONAL HYGIENE	TIME	COMMENTS

SUPPLIES NEEDED	PURCHASED	DETAILS

COMMENTS_____
_____
_____

DAILY CARE LOG

NAME OF CARER_____DATE_____
TIME BEGIN_____TIME ENDED_____
SERVICE PROVIDED_____

MEDICATION	DOSE	TIME	COMMENTS

MEALS		TIME	QUANTITY
Breakfast			
Lunch			
Teatime			
Dinner			

TIME	ACTIVITIES

PERSONAL HYGIENE	TIME	COMMENTS

SUPPLIES NEEDED	PURCHASED	DETAILS

COMMENTS_____
_____
_____

DAILY CARE LOG

NAME OF CARER_____DATE_____

TIME BEGIN_____TIME ENDED_____

SERVICE PROVIDED_____

MEDICATION	DOSE	TIME	COMMENTS

MEALS		TIME	QUANTITY
Breakfast			
Lunch			
Teatime			
Dinner			

TIME	ACTIVITIES

PERSONAL HYGIENE	TIME	COMMENTS

SUPPLIES NEEDED	PURCHASED	DETAILS

COMMENTS_____

_____

_____

DAILY CARE LOG

NAME OF CARER_____DATE_____

TIME BEGIN_____TIME ENDED_____

SERVICE PROVIDED_____

_____

MEDICATION	DOSE	TIME	COMMENTS

MEALS		TIME	QUANTITY
Breakfast			
Lunch			
Teatime			
Dinner			

TIME	ACTIVITIES

PERSONAL HYGIENE	TIME	COMMENTS

SUPPLIES NEEDED	PURCHASED	DETAILS

COMMENTS_____

_____

_____

DAILY CARE LOG

NAME OF CARER_____DATE_____
TIME BEGIN_____TIME ENDED_____
SERVICE PROVIDED_____

MEDICATION	DOSE	TIME	COMMENTS

MEALS		TIME	QUANTITY
Breakfast			
Lunch			
Teatime			
Dinner			

TIME	ACTIVITIES

PERSONAL HYGIENE	TIME	COMMENTS

SUPPLIES NEEDED	PURCHASED	DETAILS

COMMENTS_____
_____
_____

DAILY CARE LOG

NAME OF CARER_____DATE_____

TIME BEGIN_____TIME ENDED_____

SERVICE PROVIDED_____

MEDICATION	DOSE	TIME	COMMENTS

MEALS		TIME	QUANTITY
Breakfast			
Lunch			
Teatime			
Dinner			

TIME	ACTIVITIES

PERSONAL HYGIENE	TIME	COMMENTS

SUPPLIES NEEDED	PURCHASED	DETAILS

COMMENTS_____

_____

_____

DAILY CARE LOG

NAME OF CARER_____DATE_____
TIME BEGIN_____TIME ENDED_____
SERVICE PROVIDED_____

MEDICATION	DOSE	TIME	COMMENTS

MEALS		TIME	QUANTITY
Breakfast			
Lunch			
Teatime			
Dinner			

TIME	ACTIVITIES

PERSONAL HYGIENE	TIME	COMMENTS

SUPPLIES NEEDED	PURCHASED	DETAILS

COMMENTS_____
_____
_____

DAILY CARE LOG

NAME OF CARER_____DATE_____

TIME BEGIN_____TIME ENDED_____

SERVICE PROVIDED_____

MEDICATION	DOSE	TIME	COMMENTS

MEALS		TIME	QUANTITY
Breakfast			
Lunch			
Teatime			
Dinner			

TIME	ACTIVITIES

PERSONAL HYGIENE	TIME	COMMENTS

SUPPLIES NEEDED	PURCHASED	DETAILS

COMMENTS_____

_____

DAILY CARE LOG

NAME OF CARER_____DATE_____

TIME BEGIN_____TIME ENDED_____

SERVICE PROVIDED_____

MEDICATION	DOSE	TIME	COMMENTS

MEALS		TIME	QUANTITY
Breakfast			
Lunch			
Teatime			
Dinner			

TIME	ACTIVITIES

PERSONAL HYGIENE	TIME	COMMENTS

SUPPLIES NEEDED	PURCHASED	DETAILS

COMMENTS_____

_____

_____

DAILY CARE LOG

NAME OF CARER_____DATE_____
TIME BEGIN_____TIME ENDED_____
SERVICE PROVIDED_____
_____

MEDICATION	DOSE	TIME	COMMENTS

MEALS		TIME	QUANTITY
Breakfast			
Lunch			
Teatime			
Dinner			

TIME	ACTIVITIES

PERSONAL HYGIENE	TIME	COMMENTS

SUPPLIES NEEDED	PURCHASED	DETAILS

COMMENTS_____
_____
_____

DAILY CARE LOG

NAME OF CARER_____DATE_____

TIME BEGIN_____TIME ENDED_____

SERVICE PROVIDED_____

MEDICATION	DOSE	TIME	COMMENTS

MEALS		TIME	QUANTITY
Breakfast			
Lunch			
Teatime			
Dinner			

TIME	ACTIVITIES

PERSONAL HYGIENE	TIME	COMMENTS

SUPPLIES NEEDED	PURCHASED	DETAILS

COMMENTS_____

_____

_____

DAILY CARE LOG

NAME OF CARER_____DATE_____

TIME BEGIN_____TIME ENDED_____

SERVICE PROVIDED_____

_____

MEDICATION	DOSE	TIME	COMMENTS

MEALS		TIME	QUANTITY
Breakfast			
Lunch			
Teatime			
Dinner			

TIME	ACTIVITIES

PERSONAL HYGIENE	TIME	COMMENTS

SUPPLIES NEEDED	PURCHASED	DETAILS

COMMENTS_____

_____

_____

DAILY CARE LOG

NAME OF CARER_____DATE_____

TIME BEGIN_____TIME ENDED_____

SERVICE PROVIDED_____

MEDICATION	DOSE	TIME	COMMENTS

MEALS		TIME	QUANTITY
Breakfast			
Lunch			
Teatime			
Dinner			

TIME	ACTIVITIES

PERSONAL HYGIENE	TIME	COMMENTS

SUPPLIES NEEDED	PURCHASED	DETAILS

COMMENTS_____

_____

_____

DAILY CARE LOG

NAME OF CARER_____DATE_____
TIME BEGIN_____TIME ENDED_____
SERVICE PROVIDED_____
_____

MEDICATION	DOSE	TIME	COMMENTS

MEALS		TIME	QUANTITY
Breakfast			
Lunch			
Teatime			
Dinner			

TIME	ACTIVITIES

PERSONAL HYGIENE	TIME	COMMENTS

SUPPLIES NEEDED	PURCHASED	DETAILS

COMMENTS_____
_____
_____

DAILY CARE LOG

NAME OF CARER_____DATE_____

TIME BEGIN_____TIME ENDED_____

SERVICE PROVIDED_____

MEDICATION	DOSE	TIME	COMMENTS

MEALS		TIME	QUANTITY
Breakfast			
Lunch			
Teatime			
Dinner			

TIME	ACTIVITIES

PERSONAL HYGIENE	TIME	COMMENTS

SUPPLIES NEEDED	PURCHASED	DETAILS

COMMENTS_____

_____

DAILY CARE LOG

NAME OF CARER_____DATE_____
TIME BEGIN_____TIME ENDED_____
SERVICE PROVIDED_____

MEDICATION	DOSE	TIME	COMMENTS

MEALS		TIME	QUANTITY
Breakfast			
Lunch			
Teatime			
Dinner			

TIME	ACTIVITIES

PERSONAL HYGIENE	TIME	COMMENTS

SUPPLIES NEEDED	PURCHASED	DETAILS

COMMENTS_____
_____
_____

DAILY CARE LOG

NAME OF CARER_____DATE_____

TIME BEGIN_____TIME ENDED_____

SERVICE PROVIDED_____

MEDICATION	DOSE	TIME	COMMENTS

MEALS		TIME	QUANTITY
Breakfast			
Lunch			
Teatime			
Dinner			

TIME	ACTIVITIES

PERSONAL HYGIENE	TIME	COMMENTS

SUPPLIES NEEDED	PURCHASED	DETAILS

COMMENTS_____

_____

_____

DAILY CARE LOG

NAME OF CARER_____DATE_____

TIME BEGIN_____TIME ENDED_____

SERVICE PROVIDED_____

_____

MEDICATION	DOSE	TIME	COMMENTS

MEALS		TIME	QUANTITY
Breakfast			
Lunch			
Teatime			
Dinner			

TIME	ACTIVITIES

PERSONAL HYGIENE	TIME	COMMENTS

SUPPLIES NEEDED	PURCHASED	DETAILS

COMMENTS_____

_____

_____

DAILY CARE LOG

NAME OF CARER_____DATE_____
TIME BEGIN_____TIME ENDED_____
SERVICE PROVIDED_____

MEDICATION	DOSE	TIME	COMMENTS

MEALS		TIME	QUANTITY
Breakfast			
Lunch			
Teatime			
Dinner			

TIME	ACTIVITIES

PERSONAL HYGIENE	TIME	COMMENTS

SUPPLIES NEEDED	PURCHASED	DETAILS

COMMENTS_____
_____
_____

DAILY CARE LOG

NAME OF CARER_____DATE_____

TIME BEGIN_____TIME ENDED_____

SERVICE PROVIDED_____

_____

MEDICATION	DOSE	TIME	COMMENTS

MEALS			TIME	QUANTITY
Breakfast				
Lunch				
Teatime				
Dinner				

TIME	ACTIVITIES

PERSONAL HYGIENE	TIME	COMMENTS

SUPPLIES NEEDED	PURCHASED	DETAILS

COMMENTS_____

_____

_____

DAILY CARE LOG

NAME OF CARER_____DATE_____

TIME BEGIN_____TIME ENDED_____

SERVICE PROVIDED_____

MEDICATION	DOSE	TIME	COMMENTS

MEALS		TIME	QUANTITY
Breakfast			
Lunch			
Teatime			
Dinner			

TIME	ACTIVITIES

PERSONAL HYGIENE	TIME	COMMENTS

SUPPLIES NEEDED	PURCHASED	DETAILS

COMMENTS_____

_____

_____

DAILY CARE LOG

NAME OF CARER_____DATE_____

TIME BEGIN_____TIME ENDED_____

SERVICE PROVIDED_____

_____

MEDICATION	DOSE	TIME	COMMENTS

MEALS		TIME	QUANTITY
Breakfast			
Lunch			
Teatime			
Dinner			

TIME	ACTIVITIES

PERSONAL HYGIENE	TIME	COMMENTS

SUPPLIES NEEDED	PURCHASED	DETAILS

COMMENTS_____

_____

_____

DAILY CARE LOG

NAME OF CARER_____DATE_____
TIME BEGIN_____TIME ENDED_____
SERVICE PROVIDED_____

MEDICATION	DOSE	TIME	COMMENTS

MEALS		TIME	QUANTITY
Breakfast			
Lunch			
Teatime			
Dinner			

TIME	ACTIVITIES

PERSONAL HYGIENE	TIME	COMMENTS

SUPPLIES NEEDED	PURCHASED	DETAILS

COMMENTS_____
_____
_____

DAILY CARE LOG

NAME OF CARER_____DATE_____

TIME BEGIN_____TIME ENDED_____

SERVICE PROVIDED_____

MEDICATION	DOSE	TIME	COMMENTS

MEALS		TIME	QUANTITY
Breakfast			
Lunch			
Teatime			
Dinner			

TIME	ACTIVITIES

PERSONAL HYGIENE	TIME	COMMENTS

SUPPLIES NEEDED	PURCHASED	DETAILS

COMMENTS_____

_____

_____

DAILY CARE LOG

NAME OF CARER_____DATE_____
TIME BEGIN_____TIME ENDED_____
SERVICE PROVIDED_____

MEDICATION	DOSE	TIME	COMMENTS

MEALS		TIME	QUANTITY
Breakfast			
Lunch			
Teatime			
Dinner			

TIME	ACTIVITIES

PERSONAL HYGIENE	TIME	COMMENTS

SUPPLIES NEEDED	PURCHASED	DETAILS

COMMENTS_____
_____
_____

DAILY CARE LOG

NAME OF CARER_____DATE_____

TIME BEGIN_____TIME ENDED_____

SERVICE PROVIDED_____
_____

MEDICATION	DOSE	TIME	COMMENTS

MEALS		TIME	QUANTITY
Breakfast			
Lunch			
Teatime			
Dinner			

TIME	ACTIVITIES

PERSONAL HYGIENE	TIME	COMMENTS

SUPPLIES NEEDED	PURCHASED	DETAILS

COMMENTS_____
_____
_____

NOTES

DATE_____

NOTES

DATE_____

DATE_____

NOTES

DATE_____

NOTES

NOTES

DATE_____

NOTES

Made in the USA
Monee, IL
12 February 2023

27632169R00061